LIFE
LESSONS
from MISS
MATTIE

LIFE LESSONS from MISS MATTIE

RUFUS D. STEPHENS

• WRITE WAY •
PUBLISHING COMPANY
RALEIGH, NORTH CAROLINA

Life Lessons from Miss Mattie

Copyright © 2020 by Rufus D. Stephens

Printed in the United States of America
ISBN 978-1946425553

Book design by CSinclaire Write-Design
Cover design by CSinclaire Write-Design and Klevur

• WRITE WAY •
PUBLISHING COMPANY
RALEIGH, NORTH CAROLINA
www.writewaypublishingcompany.com

This book is gratefully dedicated
to my business partners and close friends,
Norm Wood and Lauren McGhee.

CONTENTS

FOREWORD

As I move through my different spaces in my life, it is becoming clear to me that it takes a village to keep the parts of my family history strong and intact for generations. As the author of *Life Lessons from Miss Mattie*, Rufus Stephens prompts us to reflect and laugh when we consider all of the characters that are infused into the word "family." Rufus guides us to think critically of our family dynamics and the messy situations that happen in every family. But together we get through them. As we enjoy the stories, he ensures that we know that in the center of the stories is a woman of God who connected herself with many people and characters to create a network of support.

This book has been in the works for decades. It brewed from short stories shared around family gatherings as Mattie's legacies spread around the country. The need to hold on to photos, memories, and hometown contacts of 46th Street neighbors became apparent to each sibling. During holidays and weekly check-in phone calls, we knew that we could not allow our history to dissolve into dust and crumpled documents. In the 1990s, Sunny began researching and tracing our family tree. Mickey gathered names and addresses of Savannah neighbors. Similarly, Laverne offered laser-focused name recollections. James kept communication moving and set up the family text messaging, and Rufus moved us all into an official writing of this narrative of recollections. Beginning with memorable family quotes which were soon woven into professional speeches and sermons, then often reflected in parties, this book has emerged.

I am fortunate to be chosen by God to be the baby of the family. As such, I have been a part of these family stories. My memories of Rufus and admiration of every phase of his life allow me to say that he is the epitome of an author for this biographical work. Writing takes intention, determination, and patience. Rufus has intended to write this book. He has had the determination and patience to move short stories into a fuller narrative of a family. Rufus centered us on this task. Now, you can reap the benefit of Miss Mattie's lessons.

Beverly Hamilton

ACKNOWLEDGMENT

After hearing a little bit about my mother, my business partners Norm Wood and Lauren McGhee encouraged me to forge ahead with writing a book about her. Norm, on many occasions and with great passion, would say, "I wanna hear more about Miss Mattie." My mother's impact had found a place in Norm's and Lauren's hearts. They missed no opportunity to encourage me to stay on point and complete the book.

Like so many, I didn't really appreciate the scope of my mother's influence until I began looking more intently at her life. We live our lives often clueless to how large and indelible a mark we leave. We can't imagine how far our reach will be. Such is the case with my mother. Decades after she had done her best work, her impact is still felt. Just the mention of her life and some of the touchpoints she made has been enough to cause others to press for greater revelations about this woman.

I am pleased to have friends whose sensitivity to and appreciation of my mother's life is so compelling. Once prompted to move ahead, I entered into this moment of writing with new passion and even greater appreciation of the incredible woman I called "Mother." Thank you, Norm and Lauren, for your loving insistence.

INTRODUCTION

I grew up in Savannah, Georgia, in a family that has outrun the statistical prophecies that were whispered about us at the time. My siblings and I grew up in a home absent of a father. My mother was a public school teacher who taught all over rural Georgia. She had a passion for education and a big heart for anyone needing a friend or a friendly face. Her very personality spoke of an uncompromising presence. It was characterized by abiding love and an ends-oriented perspective second to none.

Despite the statistical odds, it was that setting that would lay the groundwork for the emergence of the five extraordinary (I like to think) individuals my siblings and I would turn out to be. As I considered the neighborhood in which I grew up, we were among the poorest. You would not have guessed that had you visited the house that my mother, Miss Mattie Stephens, helped to build.

The provisions she made possible would all pale against the backdrop of the character building elements that would mark our progress through life. She instilled in us key principles (Life Lessons) that would enrich and influence our lives. It is my hope that the lessons learned from this book will aid others in need of the "Miss Mattie" influence in their lives.

MISS MATTIE

Five individuals who have impacted society in profound and substantive ways emerged from a single parent home in the hood. These individuals did not grow up gifted with material success on any level. If the poverty line had been established during those early years, the family would surely have been living well below it. This was my family.

The five of us, Mattie's kids as we were called, mostly lived with our grandmother in the family home in Savannah, Georgia. This is who we are by name and birth order: Robert (Sunny), Edward (Mickey), LaVerne (Bernie), Rufus (Butch), and James (Jimmy).

Our parents thought their family was complete after Bernie was born—that is until three years later when my twin James and I came along. My mother gave birth to us before ultrasound, so she knew she was having twins *when* she was having twins!

When James and I were only three and my oldest brother was eight, our parents separated. My dad was an alcoholic father, which necessarily produced in our single-source-income household a workaholic mother.

My mother was a public school teacher who

taught all over rural Georgia. Her passion for education impacted her children deeply. If you look in the dictionary for the word "unrelenting," you could find a picture of my mother. If there was something she felt was of value and worth her time, not only would she stand firm, she would press forward with it.

While her life was filled with challenges that would have crushed a lesser person, she stayed true to her mission to raise quality individuals who bore her name. Despite the statistical odds, it was that setting that would lay the groundwork for the emergence of the five strong individuals my siblings and I would turn out to be.

My mother, Ms. Mattie Stephens, provided us with all of our material needs and a few of our "wants" as well. She gave the term "mama bear" new meaning. She was tenacious and would do anything for the nurture and safety of her children.

While she made certain our material needs were met, she also provided us with things much more needful for success in life. She instilled in us eight key principles or Life Lessons that would enrich and influence the paths of our lives. As I share these Life Lessons with you, it is my sincere hope that your life path will be impacted as richly as our various paths were.

THE 1016 TRIAD

Three members of my family were responsible for our total upbringing: our grandmother Jannie, our aunt Gladys (at times, surrogate mom), and, of course, Miss Mattie. This book focuses on our intrepid mother who, as one preacher put it, would "cross hell on a spider web for her children." However, this book would never be complete without the inclusion of two people who locked arms with Miss Mattie for the benefit of her children. We all lived at 1016 W. 46th Street in Savannah, Georgia. It was the place where love lived and character was established. In an act of homage, allow me to digress to share some of their individual impacts on the five of us.

My grandmother, Jannie Dinkins, was called "Mama." It was convenient because my mother and her siblings called her "Mama." We referred to our mother as "Mother." That way no one was ever confused about who we were speaking to. As my mother pursued employment in "the country," Mama took care of the home front.

Mama was an incredible grandmother. She loved easily and deeply. Her repeated prayer was that she would get to see each of her grandchildren graduate from high school. She was blessed to see all of us attend college.

Mama impacted us in three significant ways that come to mind whenever I think of her. I could call her a great cook though that would be a gross understatement. She could be more correctly described as an awesome meal creator. She would take the most meager of supplies and create a sumptuous meal from them.

I often remember her giving me whatever change she may have had in her purse to get something for her to cook for dinner. I remember going to the store with 17 cents to purchase loose rice. If you know anything about rice, you know a little goes a long way. Whether for breakfast or dinner, biscuits were a staple in our house. She would whip up a pan of biscuits in a heartbeat.

As a part of a 4-H project I raised chickens. I had 48 Rhode Island Red hens and 2 very happy roosters. I raised them and won blue ribbons at the county fair. Afterwards, they would lay large double yoke eggs daily. We never needed to buy eggs. In fact, I sold eggs to several women in the neighborhood who baked.

Then something happened that I hadn't anticipated. Somewhere along the way as I prospered as an egg salesman, I discovered girls. I dropped egg sales and my affection for my chickens like a bad habit. That decision worked well for my grandmother's food supply plan.

We systematically killed and ate every chicken off the yard over the course of a year or so. She would tell me to get this or that one, and it was done. I was the executioner and dresser of the chickens. The last act of poultry supply was directed toward the two roosters. When dressed, Mama made them into chicken salad. Life was good!

The second way she impacted us was as an unlicensed healthcare professional. It really didn't matter what the illness or medical need was, Mama was up to the challenge. My twin suffered with severe asthma attacks during the winter. My grandmother fought that illness like it was an intruder, and James always recovered well. We all suffered bad colds, insect stings, and a host of accidents. She would make us take horrible tasting medicine like Castor Oil and other concoctions. She was laser-focused when it came to us taking the worst thing ever invented to go into someone's mouth. We would often have to drink what we called sassafras tea as an elixir. I will admit that after a day of "treatment" we were much better, and the cold had passed.

Occasionally, my grandmother would reach out to a neighborhood friend for a particular homemade remedy she was fond of using. It was routinely referred to as "Aunt Rhaney's Salve." Mama would rub this questionable salve on our chests to help us breathe better. I have to say this salve would put Vick's VapoRub™ to shame.

One day, out of curiosity, I read the directions on the little bottle. It said, "Good for toothaches and pneumonia." I just shook my head and continued to trust my grandmother. There was never a time when my grandmother didn't meet our medical needs. While I praise her skills, I celebrate the love that drove those skills. You could not be touched by Mama without feeling profound love as she did what love called her to do.

The last way my grandmother impacted us was

with her loving personality. She loved everyone associated with our house. It was hard to be around her and not be prompted to love more or lead with your heart in some specific situation. She always looked for the best in everyone.

I have watched her walk in love on so many occasions. She always felt love was a better option in just about everything we did.

However, while she was loving, she was no one's doormat. For those of you who see niceness as implied permission for bad behavior, be forewarned. One thing you don't want to do is take nice people "there." I promise you, when they get "there," you won't recognize them. *Let nice people be nice!*

The second part of The Triad was our aunt, Gladys Roberts. She was my mother's sister and my grandmother's middle child. Incredible seems an appropriate word to describe her as well. She was a surrogate mother, there for all of us whenever she was needed. She disciplined us without hesitation because the love relationship allowed for it. And she laughed easily and encouraged us to laugh too. I don't know where the name came from, but we often called her "Chicken." When I think of her, I think of warm smiles, professionalism, classiness, and encouragement.

Gladys was a registered nurse and public school educator. She always presented herself in a polished fashion. Anyone else could be casual; it would never be her. Like everyone else in our family line, she met no strangers. She was ever the encourager, especially where education was concerned.

If she happened to live in another city, we would often stay with her for days and, in some cases, the school year. I was in her class in third grade and lived with her. She honored her mother by perfecting kitchen skills, and I was the grateful beneficiary of some awesome meals.

When she visited Savannah, she would always stay with us and was a seamless part of the whole family. She would often regale us with her life exploits. She spent a lot of time in New York City where she worked as a nurse. I remember being mesmerized by her New York stories. In many ways, my aunt Gladys aided my mother in establishing the "possibility factor" in the five of us. "Chicken" was a wonderful and much loved member of the 1016 Triad.

Since the majority of this book is about the third member of the member of the Triad, Miss Mattie, I will close this section by sharing with you the innerworkings of these awesome women. My mother and her sister, Gladys, honored their mother and were always ready to meet her needs. They could often be seen working in tandem on behalf of some project. Sometimes it would be preparing a huge meal for some holiday. Other times, it would involve us preparing to go on a road trip. When they joined forces, as they often did, the five of us were the grateful recipients of their synergy.

LIFE LESSON 1

EDUCATION IS NON-NEGOTIABLE

LIFE LESSON 1

"Education is the key to success in life, and teachers make a lasting impact in the lives of their students."
Solomon Ortiz

Education Is Non-negotiable — *You* will *go to school!*

From as early as I can remember, education was an important watchword for our family. In order for African American families to make any type of socio-economic headway, education is critically important. My mother knew that and insisted on good education for each of us.

It did not matter to her that the books we received throughout elementary and high school were the torn and tattered leftovers from the students at white schools. The tattered and torn books collected at the end of the school year and sent to the black schools made room for the brand new books the white schools would receive.

I remember reading names like *Billy Witkowsky* and *Sarah O'Connor* written in many of my "new" books. My siblings and I realized that we could learn from the other students' cast offs and move forward. Whining was never allowed!

My mother taught school throughout rural Georgia in more towns than I can count. My earliest recollections are of my mother, my older brother, Mickey, and me in a two-room school near a rural town called Horse Creek in Georgia.

We boarded with a local farmer who lived less than a mile from the school. There were only two teachers in the school. One teacher, my teacher, taught grades one through three, and my mother taught grades four through seven, the class my brother was in.

This scene would repeat itself at several schools and at several boarding houses throughout Georgia as my mother provided the educational foundation for so many students. The mission was two-fold for her: teach their kids and teach her kids. She would teach and nurture others as she taught and nurtured us.

Wherever my mother taught, she was highly regarded. We would make home visits from time to time. She was always received warmly and greeted with a "Hey Miss Steve, get out and come in!" I have thought about those days often, and I have come to one solid conclusion. My mother was a social animal and really loved people, which made it easy for them to love her. While all of that existed, the real telling point was that she represented hope in the community.

She represented something greater than lives filled with menial jobs and low self-esteem as personal destinies. My mother represented possibility! Her passion for education created a vehicle of hope.

My mother deeply loved her five children and enjoyed being around us. But her teaching jobs took her away from Savannah and that would necessitate her separation from us.

She would try to counteract that by taking some of us to go to school wherever she happened to be teaching that school year. Some of us would see much of our elementary school years with her. Others would spend their junior high and high school years at other Miss Mattie destinations.

The great thing about the many Miss Mattie touchpoints was just that—she was there. She, and those of us with her, touched the lives of many and were touched by them as well. Not only did we receive our Miss Mattie imposed educations but we also formed friendships that would last for decades. My mother would have said that *that* was the great serendipity of getting our educations.

My mother was fully invested in teaching. She was an avid reader and encouraged reading for each of us. My mother loved words. Some words could paint better pictures than others, and we received repeated examples of her great word choices.

Expanding on the education thought, college education was important to my mother. She graduated from college, and she fully expected no less from her children. The day would come when life would challenge her passion for education. Her oldest three children where stair-step kids. So, for at least two years, she would have three children in college at the same time. This was at a time when she earned very little as an educator.

But Miss Mattie was up for the challenge. She often had a second job. Sometimes she worked as a server at a local restaurant. When she wasn't doing that, she would find herself cleaning offices at a nearby military base. When her physical efforts just weren't enough, she would resort to borrowing money from a local high-interest finance company. For Miss Mattie, nothing, absolutely nothing, would stop her children from getting an education.

My siblings and I all felt the determined prompt of our mother to go to school, to learn, and to become productive and significant citizens in society. As it turned out, we would each complete high school and then go on to attend college. Three of the five of us would earn graduate degrees.

This, as you can imagine, made Miss Mattie very proud. She rarely missed an opportunity to brag on her five kids. To her, it was worth all of the backbreaking jobs she held to fund her children's education, all the sermons on education she delivered to us, and the occasional confrontation with one of us about doing anything other than going to school. Her words still echo in my head, "You *will* go to school! And we did indeed go to school.

If my mother could sit down with you now and give you a word of advice guaranteed to enhance your life, whatever your age, she would say, *"Get some education!"* She would not necessarily be talking about a high school diploma or college degree. She would tell you to acquire education that would give you knowledge and make you better able to impact the society you live in.

We live in an age where educational content abounds. There is no reason for anyone not to expand the boundaries of their education. What are you doing to increase your knowledge in some area? The ball is in your court. Get smart! Learn new things!

LIFE LESSON 2

SELF-IMAGE

LIFE LESSON 2

"You have Greatness within you."
Les Brown

Self-Image — *Remember, you are something else!*

As I recall the early years of my upbringing, I remember constant assaults on my self-image. When we were young, peer assaults were daily occurrences. Whatever it was that you didn't like about yourself, someone would use it as their springboard for assault. Those kinds of playground attacks were just part of growing up. Every generation has its "time in the barrel."

There was an even greater assault that was leveled against not just my family but against all black families. It was more sinister and, at times, openly hostile.

There was the systematic discounting of black people throughout the country and especially in the South. The "white only" water fountains and bathrooms were everywhere.

We were not allowed to get food at the same

counters as whites as we were considered inferior. If we wanted food from many establishments, we would have to get it at the back door.

This ethnic discounting was everywhere.

Both the playground assaults and the ethnic discounting could and often did show up in the lives of many in the form of self-loathing, that inner discounting that needed no further prompting.

I developed areas in my life that caused me to have a poor self-image. Although I was one of the youngest of my siblings, I was the largest in physical stature. In a most unflattering manner, I was often referred to as "big head."

Through all this, I always knew where I could go for "better" input. Miss Mattie, alternately "Dr. Mattie," would have just the medicine I needed. She would quickly remind me that I was big all over and that I was very special. She would help me wage war against my enemies of self-discount.

Ms. Mattie often reminded all of us how great we were. It did not matter that we didn't have a father in the house as so many of our friends had. It didn't matter that we didn't have many of the material things our friends had. We were comforted and encouraged by the directed love and reassurances of those who reared us. I've already written about the other two members of what I call "The Triad" who joined forces in the rearing of "Mattie's kids." We were frequently reminded of the greatness of our heritage.

My grandfather, my mother's father, set the drumbeat for the rich legacy that would follow him. My grandfather, Rufus J. Dinkins, was an incredible man. He pastored a local church until his death. He powerfully touched so many lives in and out of his local assembly. He strived for excellence in his life and expected the same from my mother and her two siblings. I look very much like him; he was an incredibly handsome man!

I rarely went anywhere when someone didn't say something kind about my grandfather. He passed away in 1946, but when I spoke at the Georgia House of Representative about five years ago, my grandfather's name was brought up in very kind fashion. He married an equally loving person in our grandmother, Jannie, with whom we lived. Her loving influence on each of us cannot be overstated.

This is all to say that my siblings and I came into this world fully equipped for whatever life had to offer. My mother lost no time in reminding us of our personal greatness. While we were all from one family, we were each distinct, unique, and with our own special place on the world stage.

My mother carried herself in a fashion that demanded respect. She respected herself and would accept nothing less from others. Even when we were at our lowest materially, you could never tell from Miss Mattie's countenance. She modeled self-respect to us in such a way that we fully understood the difference between what we had and who we were.

I wish each of you reading this book could feel the great joy I felt when my mother emphatically reminded me of my own greatness. No one sang praises like Miss Mattie, but I will try for you: *You are indeed something else!*

LIFE LESSON 3

LAUGH REGULARLY

LIFE LESSON 3

"Always find a reason to laugh. It may not add years to your life, but it will add life to your years."
LiveLifeHappy.com

Laugh Regularly — *Life is funny!*

It's Saturday morning at 1016 W. 46th Street in Savannah. My mother is on the front porch laughing loudly with a neighbor from across the street. She has either prompted someone's funny bone or they have hers. Either way, the result was the same; she laughed heartily.

With all of the negativity around her, my mother could have resorted to the thumb-sucking and self-pity of the defeated. Such a possibility was never in my mother. God enhanced her DNA with a funny factor. It was from her that we learned to laugh—not so politely sometimes in our exuberance. Because of my mother, I often find myself reduced to tears of laughter. Someone said, *"Sometimes I laugh so hard, the tears run down my legs."* It could easily have been my mother who said that.

I realized early on in my life that there was something very special about my Mattie-led family. I noticed this capacity for laughter in all of my siblings. Laughter came easily and with great regularity to all of us.

It appears that Miss Mattie was ahead of her time. Researchers and clinicians have proven repeatedly the value of laughter in our lives. There are significant therapeutic upsides to laughter. While my mother would not have known any of that, she knew that she was better for intentionally losing herself in laughing, and she imparted the same philosophy to all of us.

Realizing that it was such an intrinsic part of my existence, I explored this idea of laughing from a benefits perspective. Most notably I can see that laughter has tempered my perspective on the serious things of life.

Understand that I'm not reducing the painful, unsettling things of life to silliness. What I am saying is that I see painful and unsettling events as much less sinister and crushing than I did in the past. Laughter truly has a curative effect. It helps me heal from emotional events more quickly.

Losing my wife in June of 1995 and 60 days later losing my mother was devastating. My wife, Lillian, had been my best friend since 10th grade. We had been married for 24 years and had two teenage daughters when she lost her battle with cancer. I was in a state of disorientation that I could never have imagined. Even in that state, it was the memories of the hysterically funny times we shared that kept me. It was much the same when my mother passed. Again, the memories were rich and full of humor. Finding laughter played an integral part in keeping me centered through this unsettling time in my life.

Another benefit from allowing laughter into my life is relationship building. There is something about me which I didn't invent and don't intentionally try to use for relationship building that seems to affect people in a great way. I believe people are more trusting and open with me and my messages because of my sincere humorous side. Let the laughter that is a part of your identity be part of future relationships in your life.

I am sure that my mother used laughter to help her weather the storms of life that blew into her world with some degree of regularity. It was not easy raising three stair-step children at one time. In April of 1946, when the oldest was three years old and the youngest was one, another storm would visit my mother's life.

My mother was a "daddy's girl," and her very foundations were rocked when her father, the Rev. Rufus J. Dinkins, died on a trip to Baltimore, Maryland. His appendix burst during the train ride, and he died, in large part, because he was not allowed to be treated at the white hospital in Baltimore. Miss Mattie was not unacquainted with grief and life challenges. She clearly functioned with an intentional focus on the brighter side of life. My mother's unstated philosophy of life has become my mantra, *"Life will give us everything we need to cry about, so we must take the opportunity to run after every laugh moment we can find."*

My acquaintance with laughter had an early genesis. When I was about six or seven years old, I remember riding in a car full of my mother's teacher friends making their weekly 63-mile trip from Savannah where they all lived to Sylvania where they all taught. I don't remember what I said in my innocence, but whatever it was, it caused everyone in the car to erupt with laughter. They, with my mother leading the pack, laughed so hard they had to pull the car over until they collected themselves and could drive on.

Now, as a grown man, I frequently chase after a laughter moment, fully understanding the upside value of doing so. I often listen to favorite comedians or hang around people with a pronounced sense of humor to keep my funny bone engaged.

I would challenge you to do some introspection where laughter is concerned. Do you find yourself far too serious most of the time? Do you ever take time to laugh? Seek things that bring you happiness. Experience the joy of laughing. Once you have done that, then intentionally look for other laugh opportunities and lose yourself in them. They're everywhere. Laughter is a wonderful tool for a happy existence. Miss Mattie would simply say to you, *"Laugh!"*

LIFE LESSON 4

ENCOURAGEMENT

LIFE LESSON 4

"There is no exercise better for the heart than reaching down and lifting people up."
– John Holmes

Encouragement — *We are blessed to bless others.*

The Miss Mattie Life Lesson that has most affected me is "Encouragement." Not only has it affected me, it has emerged as one of the reasons I exist. The world is filled with haters, naysayers, and those who will never see you above your current circumstances. Our home was a home where encouragement loomed large.

My mother always had some student she was helping. She would bring them home for the weekend, and they would shadow her and be encouraged by her. Looking back, it is quite amusing that they would find our surroundings so great. At times we had seven people living in a three bedroom house and all four boys slept in one bedroom in the back. Sometimes at night it sounded like an episode of the *Three Stooges* with all of the snoring, snorts, and unmentionable sounds.

But my mother's charges found our home palatial. It was my mother's way of encouraging even the lowliest of her students/mentees and reminding them of their greatness. My brothers and I, for very selfish reasons, loved it when our mother would bring some of her girl students home. Echoing Forrest Gump, *"That's all I have to say about that."*

One of Miss Mattie's students showed up at my mother's funeral and proclaimed Miss Mattie opened up possibilities in her life. This former student of some 25 years earlier stood and said, "I have a Mercedes parked in the parking lot of this church. That was made possible because of Miss Mattie." Encouragement was one of my mother's watchwords.

Miss Mattie's encouragement could be seen in many venues. I played pony league baseball when I was in my teens. One day when we were playing an important game, I came to bat. The bases were loaded and, you guessed it, I hit a homerun—grand slam! I was a lefty, and I hit the ball to left field down the third base line. The left fielder played me as a pull hitter and had to run hard to get the ball. That allowed me enough time to clear the bases.

The other three runners had made it home. Coming from second to third, my coach gave me the signal to head for home. As I rounded third base, there was my mother jumping up and down like she was a 45-year-old member of my personal pom squad. I can still hear her yelling, "Go, Butch, Go!" When I touched home, I was covered by my teammates—and my mother!

She was no less encouraging of my siblings. Each of my siblings can give graphic accounts of our mother's encouragement in their lives. While we were all pretty good kids, we were still young folk with issues. My mother's words and acts of encouragement were both necessary and without limits.

It was Christmas week and I was in the fifth grade. This was one of the years when I spent the school year with my mother. It was made more interesting because I was in her class. This particular week was very special. It was the week that all of us as students would present the teacher (my mom) with a Christmas gift.

I had saved for some time to buy a pink glass powder holder I had seen at the local 5 & 10 cent store (as they were called then). The lid of the round powder holder was a French poodle. It could not have cost more than $5.00. It felt like I paid $1,000 for it. I would look at it from time to time and say, "She's gonna love this!"

I was so excited when the morning arrived when we were supposed to present our gifts to our teacher. At the top of the stairs my mother and I had to climb to go our class, I tripped and the package carrying my precious gift, my "$1,000" gift, hit the concrete. The sound of my package hitting the pavement confirmed that the gift had broken into many pieces. I gasped, hardly able to breathe. And then I began to sob. I was a ten-year-old boy whose great hope of making his mother, his best friend, smile was dashed on the unforgiving concrete of the stairs.

Even to this point in my life, there have been very few times when I have been hurt more. My mother, ever the encourager, rushed into action. Her warm words found the needy places in my heart and helped to bring me back from the edge of despair even when the other students were presenting their gifts to her. Miss Mattie let me know I'd be all right, and I was still loved.

In our attempts toward personal happiness and success, we too often run right past opportunities to encourage people. My mother's influence around encouragement still lives on in me. Encouragement has become one of my "why's" in life, and it drives my desire to be a motivational speaker. The Good Book reminds us that there is "power in the tongue." This relatively small body part that we use for talking, swallowing, and licking ice cream is incredibly powerful.

I learned years ago that I can change people's disposition by saying what others are afraid to say or do not take the time to say. When we fail to issue "good words" because the person receiving them might be uncomfortable and embarrassed, we miss an opportunity to uplift. When we rush and do not acknowledge someone's efforts, we miss the opportunity to show sincere appreciation. When we do not offer praise because we don't know what words to use, a simple, heartfelt "good job" or "thank you" delivered with a smile can elevate your mood and theirs!

I have found any small embarrassment of being singled out for praise always to be eclipsed by the joy and appreciation of the compliment. I can still see in my mind's eye the faces of many people I have spoken encouragingly to. From a quick dimple reveal to a full out smile and a hearty thank you, the "good words" are always welcomed.

In 2015, I lived in the Chicago area and in my retirement, I decided to drive Uber. I have always loved interfacing with people. On one occasion, I had been talking with a young lady in her twenties who was concerned about her life. I shifted into encouragement mode—I had had plenty of experience with my own young adult kids. We continued riding for about twenty minutes, and I encouraged her each mile of the way. When we neared her PricewaterhouseCoopers destination on Wacker Drive, she said with an improved spirit, "This is like a therapy car. Can you pick me up every morning?" We both laughed, and I wished her well.

On another Uber occasion, I picked up a fifty-year-old passenger who was heading for Michigan Avenue. He gave his family big hugs before we headed out. He asked me what I did, and I told him that I was a professional speaker. I told him that one of my signature messages was "50 . . . Now What?"

He was intrigued when I told him that the central theme was to challenge people not to write themselves off simply because they had gotten older. I pointed out to him the irony of affecting an "age shutdown" at that point in life where we have never had as many life experiences, never been smarter, and never been wiser than we are right then. We are full of assets and should be seeking outlets to apply those assets.

He paused for a minute and said, "Rufus, I was meant to ride with you today." He told me that he was a successful businessman and had taken very good care of his family. He mentioned that his lucrative position came at a cost, however. He traveled a lot and, more importantly, he had neglected one of his passion points. He said he had been working on an invention that would be a significant help to our society and would be quite profitable. Then he said again, "Rufus, I was meant to ride with you today."

I believe I have been gifted and Mattie-influenced with great speaking abilities. That makes speaking encouragement easy for me. Many of you reading this book have the same gifting. I would challenge you to use it more often. Your words don't have to be profound, just encouraging. Consider this. There will be the cashier who feels beat-up because insensitive and rude people have made a mess of her day. There will be that support person who never hears a good word about his work. Situations like these spell opportunity for you. You can change their paradigm for the moment, maybe for the day—maybe for longer—with some good words. Don't miss the opportunity.

Encouragement comes in flavors other than speaking. There is also great power in the written word. Try this when you get a chance. Write a three or four sentence note to someone you care about or who has done something nice for someone or who seems like they are having a hard day.

Say something encouraging in the note. Remind them of what they mean to you, mention the good thing they did, offer a compliment on a small accomplishment, thank them for something, or anything else of an uplifting nature. Don't walk up and present it to them in some grand gesture; your presence will get in the way. Leave the note where they will find it or drop it in the mail. I promise you that your note will do its work.

One of the things that I have come to value is that life is all about touchpoints. No doubt this is influenced by my mother who touched so many lives. Each of us should touch as many lives as we can as we pass through our journey. Miss Mattie would tell us that that is the way to spell "encouragement."

I remember a bit of a different kind of touchpoint

from years ago. Older people in our community had a distinct way of showing material encouragement. If they were going to give you $20 because you needed it, they would never showboat. They respected your pride, and they didn't want to expose your need to people around. They would grab your hand to shake it and palm a twenty-dollar bill into your hand, often with a warm smile of confirmation. My mother was one such person.

Now here is a huge takeaway. I learned early on this fact about encouragement. The greater benefit is often to the giver and not to the one receiving. I love to actively practice encouraging, often in dramatic Miss Mattie fashion, and I am immediately rewarded with a company of warm emotions. It's about the connection. Try it! You'll be all the better for your efforts.

LIFE LESSON 5

STAND FIRM

LIFE LESSON 5

"I come as One, I stand as Ten Thousand."
Maya Angelou

Stand Firm — *Stand for something or you'll fall for anything!*

"Fighting Mattie Dinkins" was what my mother was called growing up in grade school. She was not likely to start a fight, but if you took her there, she'd surely meet you there. She was a PK, a preacher's kid. As such, she was held to unrealistic standards by adults and received on-going taunts from her peers. Because she was "raised right," she could do nothing about the adults. On the other hand, she was ready, willing, and able to handle her peers. Nothing good would likely come out of a skirmish with Mattie. She would also tell us that sometimes when she wasn't dealing with her own issues, she helped her sister, Gladys, clean up a messy situation that Gladys may have been involved in.

She never made it a habit of losing many battles.

That would turn out to be a pattern that would guide her life. She saw ordeals just as things she had to deal with. She would caution us not to give ordeals more respect than they deserved. I am convinced that her fighting spirit aided her significantly in navigating the challenging waters of her own life.

Like many things in my mother's life, if a character trait was worth living, it was worth teaching to her kids. After all, those five babies owned her heart. She taught us all to stand firm against the things of life that wanted to diminish our self-esteem and disrupt our well-being. Sometimes she would stand with us, and other times, we would have to go it on our own with her background guidance.

Many of us had to deal with bullies and play-ground extortionists in grade school. My mother would assure us that if we didn't stand up against our bullies, we would have to face her when we got home. We were forced by the prospects of facing Miss Mattie to face our adversaries.

That would serve us well when the time came for each of us to face more sinister adversaries in life. Her "Stand!" directives sang through my head when academic challenges showed up in my life to see what I was made of. We would be reminded to "Stand!" when financial distress found our driveways. When marital challenges invaded our life spaces, we were challenged to "Stand!" When health issues threatened to unravel our well-being, we were challenged to "Stand!" When opposition, however defined, raised itself against us, "Stand!" would be our watchword.

There is an old saying, "You can't lead where you won't go and you can't teach what you don't know." My mother could have coined that quote. She challenged us to "Stand" because she had in fact stood, and she knew the upside benefits of assuming that role. She led us and she taught us well.

She stood against fellow educators, both high school and college, when it appeared to her that grade assignments were capricious and driven by ill will. She stood against merchants in the marketplace who routinely discounted blacks in their dealings with us. She even stood against us, the five she loved, when we acted like someone not raised by her and the other two members of The Triad.

Because she had heart attachment with us, her "Stand" was formidable and without opposition. We yielded! Yes, for benefit of our own preservation, we yielded.

In my life alone, I have faced many challenges. We are all products of our own decisions. I have made many decisions that have not served me well. A little more thought mixed with a bit of wisdom would have served me so much better on some of those decisions.

There is nothing like living in the consequences of your own making. In 1981, after living in Illinois for 11 years, I decided to return to Savannah to live. That decision was one of the heart and not of the head. For two and a half years, I would live emotionally and materially diminished. I earned a little better than a third of my earnings in Illinois.

My position as breadwinner was put to the test. I had to "Stand." At one point, I found myself getting up at four a.m. to deliver the morning paper throughout the city. I was Standing.

When I wasn't doing that, I found myself hosting

at a local Savannah restaurant called The Pirates House. I was Standing. My Standing, in this case, took on another form when my sixth grade teacher walked in the restaurant for lunch one day. Her name was Delores Washington, and I had not seen her since I was eleven years old and had a crush on her. I took a deep breath and allowed my heart to re-start. I was thirty-five years old and still feeling the effects of my crush.

I said, "Hello, ladies, welcome to The Pirates House." She never missed a beat. She said, "Hello, Stephens." It was all I could do to physically stand. It had been 24 years and she still remembered me. I made my mother proud; I stood!

There is no better posture for self-satisfaction and core confidence than Standing when adversity or difficult times, whatever they look like, visit you. Standing positions you for the next curve ball in life, and it makes it so much easier to look in the mirror at the woman whose hair you comb or the man whose face you shave.

If my mother was your friend or acquaintance, she would surely hold your feet to the fire when it came to Standing. As she did with her children, she would often Stand with you.

As the issues of life come to visit, you would do well to adopt this lesson from Miss Mattie and simply Stand. The demons of self-doubt, past negative history, and the ever-present sideline haters will seek to convince you that "resistance is futile." But let the Lesson from Miss Mattie sing in your head and just STAND.

LIFE LESSON 6

FAITH HAS FEET

LIFE LESSON 6

"All things are possible to him who believes."
– Mark 9:23

Faith Has Feet — *God Ain't Sleep.*

My mother was the youngest daughter of a Baptist preacher at Tremont Temple Baptist Church in Savannah. She was raised in the church and played piano for several choirs. This was also the training ground for my mother to develop her singing ability. By the time my twin and I came along, that voice was well developed, and we were treated often to the melodies of her rich alto voice.

While all of us do not follow the same faith path, I want to tell you a little about Miss Mattie's. This is simply a statement of what was, and still is, regarding Miss Mattie's and her children's faith walks.

Her faith in Christ was established early on. Both her parents walked in strong faith and encouraged their children and grandchildren to walk in faith as well. My mother's faith was nurtured further through Christian education, and faith became a way of life for her as she grew older. She would need that grounding when life would confront her many times with its agenda of destabilization, disruption, hurt, fear, and pain.

My mother trusted God to meet her and her family's needs. Her faith was tested when she found herself a single mother of five with the oldest being eight. That situation was made worse because she still loved my father.

Her faith was tested to a point I can only imagine when she received the horrific notice of her much-loved father's death as he traveled to Maryland. They shared a very special attachment. Miss Mattie had children one, two, and three years of age at the time. Nothing but faith would help her keep it together.

Her faith would be further tested when several of her children became seriously ill from time to time. There is a special desperation reserved only for mothers who have to weather the storm of very sick babies. Miss Mattie never wilted. Friends and family were ever-present, but it was her faith in God that kept her.

When she decided to venture out of Savannah to teach in rural Georgia, faith was always at the ready. She would have to convince many would-be landlords to allow her and one or two of her children to board with them for the school year. Sometimes we lived in town. Other times we lived with a farmer who happened to have the extra room that would accommodate us.

Faith would be needed to make the 63-mile trip between Sylvania and Savannah every week. We would often make the trip at night and that had its own kind of trepidation for us.

There is nothing like country darkness. The absence of ground lighting makes it a special kind of darkness. The kind of darkness where you can't see your hand in front of your face. It was the kind of darkness that made you pray that the car would never have a problem and that we would never find ourselves on the side of the road. I should also mention that this was in the 50s and 60s, and racial tensions were still issues of concern.

Miss Mattie would need extraordinary faith to muster the courage and energy to go down to the local finance company to get one of several high-interest loans she would need for college tuitions. With three children in college at the same time, and one of them out of state, I can only imagine what that was like. Faith was another watchword for her. She counted on God to keep her in those frightening times that we, as her children, never saw on her face.

Someone said, "I would rather see a sermon than hear one." Our mother often referred to God, and she loved the scriptures, but she never preached to us. She modeled Christian character for us. She modeled faith like no one I know. Integrity was serious business for my mother. She had no patience with lying, cheating, or stealing. Such character flaws were met head-on and dealt with swiftly.

Once, when I was in my teens, I collected a bag of pecans from a neighbor's yard. The problem? I had not asked the neighbor for them. I came home excited about my new found "pecan riches" and met my mother at the door. She asked where I had gotten them, and I told her. The next question would spell indictment for me!

She asked me if I had asked the neighbor if I could

have them. When I said, "No," her face morphed into that of a woman who was not pleased. It was a face I recognized from previous bad behavior encounters. She immediately chewed me out about "stealing" and told me to go back to the neighbor's house, ring the doorbell, and tell them that I had stolen their pecans. After that, I was to take that bag of pecans and spread them all over the neighbor's yard where I had found them.

She introduced us all to church at early ages. For years we were made to go to church with her, and then, at some point, we were free to choose where we wanted to go to church. We went in many different faith directions, but regardless of the church banner, faith in God was a part of our individual economies.

Our grandmother Jannie was much more demonstrative about religion and her life in Christ. We never ate breakfast on Sundays until she had prayed for the meal and her household. Sometimes the prayers were so long, the grits got cold. My grandmother loved the Lord. My mother's faith was formed to some significant degree by her mother who lived her faith daily.

Faith and trust in God were evident in everything around our house. There were times when food was scarce, but it never swayed our grandmother's or our mother's faith. That faith was often rewarded by kind material gifts from friends of our family. Sometimes it was the kindness of a family friend who worked in the school lunchroom and who brought leftovers from the school lunch program served earlier that day.

Where religion is concerned in my family, we don't all practice our faiths with the same passion, but faith on some level still drives our lives. The seeds of faith planted by our mother and grandmother have taken root and serve us well to this day.

My mother's and grandmother's faiths led me to Christ where I have found strength, confidence, solace, encouragement, and hope. I could tell you of many times that I have had to trust God because my devices and schemes had failed me miserably. And I can tell that in every case that faith was validated. I am better for having trusted God.

Faith can move mountains!

LIFE LESSON 7

SEASON YOUR SPEECH

LIFE LESSON 7

"The tongue can paint what the eyes can't see."
– Chinese Proverb

Season Your Speech — *Say it with color.*

My mother was the quintessential wordsmith. She loved the power of words. Why say it casually when you could say it with color and deliberateness. For example, a friend would ask her, *"Mattie, how are you doing today?"* If it was one of those mediocre, uneventful days, she could have said like almost everyone else, *"I'm doing OK."* Or *"So, so."* But that would be far too easy and too colorless for my mother. Depending on who it was who asked the question, her answer would be, *"Kicking, not too high. Fluttering, still can't fly."*

She understood the power of colorful speech. Colorful speech paints pictures that facilitate comprehension and often prompts people to buy into an idea you have been promoting. It flavors conversations with a richness that would otherwise be lost. It lays the ground for remembering what was said. Colorful speech also provides greater and more ready recall. It can often provide a conversational environment where humor finds a home.

Miss Mattie understood all of this, although she may not have stated it as definitively. She honed her craft and became an excellent conversationalist. She spoke while infusing messages with colorful, impactful references. A case in point—one February day a friend asked her, *"Mattie, how're you doing?"* and she said, *"If I can just February, I will certainly March."* In addition to making great word choices, she loved to do plays on words.

While these were humorous references to my mother's use of words, she used words quite articulately in serious situations as well. She often used words surgically to address inequities involving her beloved children and others for whom she became a self-appointed crusader.

Neither her love nor her skill for colorful wording has been lost on her children. I am often told that I have a great use of words. I have heard that most of my adult life. My oldest brother, Robert, reminded me that it was, in fact, a gift from our mother. I had written him a letter and used what I now realize was "Mattie speak," and he recognized it.

I love making deliberate and colorful word choices. I have been rewarded repeatedly for doing so. It has fueled my speaking career like nothing else has. As a storyteller, word choices are critical to the story's impact on the listeners. The words don't have to be big, polysyllabic words. Sometimes the smaller words carry greater weight and more flavor.

One of the things that has aided my speech has been reading and, of course, listening to colorful speakers, whether on TV, radio, or in person. When you hear a word that you don't recognize, don't run away from it. Pause for a minute and write it out if you can. I always stop and look it up—it's easy now with Google! If I like the word and the definition works for me, I use the word in a sentence as quickly and often as possible until it becomes mine and shows up in casual and formal conversations and written communication.

Miss Mattie would add a warning about seasoning your speech. She would remind you that colorful speech is not effective if it's not understood. In some people's quest to speak in a colorful manner, they choose words that people don't know. They may sound educated and impressive, but they will not have communicated. Keep it simple.

Let me give you an example. Suppose I ran up to you breathless, hands on my knees trying to breathe, and said to you, "A conflagration is consuming your abode!" You might rightfully respond, "What are you talking about?" Wouldn't it be better if I simply said to you, "Your house is on fire!" Same message, but the second time it was understood. Keep it simple!

When you season your speech, you make yourself memorable. Many people have speech patterns that resemble warm ice cream or lukewarm coffee. Those listening to them are ever hopeful of a short-lived conversation. Decide right now that you will not be numbered among those employing warm ice cream or lukewarm coffee speech patterns.

Miss Mattie would advise you to "season your speech" and say it, whatever "it" is, with color in words that can be understood!

LIFE LESSON 8—A BONUS LESSON

Live Intentionally

LIFE LESSON 8—A BONUS LESSON

*"Carve your name on hearts, not tombstones.
A legacy is etched into the minds of others
and the stories they share about you."*
Shannon Adler

Live Intentionally — *Leave a mark.*

My mother was as intentional about living her life as she was about nearly everything. The incomparable Quincy Jones said, "They're gonna know we came through here." That quote could have been my mother's mission statement. She lived life on purpose and with the expectation that her impact would not be easily forgotten. Mission accomplished.

My mother never did anything casually. Her thought was that if it was worth doing, then it was to be done well and with indelible impact. We should always leave a mark. In Quincy's words, someone should know "we came through here."

My mother was not interested in some showy,

self-absorbed posture that no one appreciated except the one doing it. She intended for us to make meaningful interactions (marks) with people. Marks that benefited them more than us. How good are you at leaving marks?

Let's consider some reasons for leaving marks. Here are four great reasons for us to leave them:

- Someone needs the inspiration that your mark will provide. We should leave a mark because we are all interdependent. Your mark may be a simple word of encouragement or a compliment on something you have noticed someone say or do. They need to hear from you.

- We can change people's well-being. We can change their dispositions for the better. And when their dispositions change for the better, their actions can change for the better. So we, in effect, become change agents just by "leaving a mark."

- We can cause people to see the world in a significantly different way than they ever have before. Some act on your part can impact someone so dramatically that they process the world and its people for the better.

- Finally, we can cause people to acknowledge the greatness that's within them. Often, people are too close to their own greatness. Because of that, they take themselves for granted. A mark left by you can help them shift their focus. They begin to appreciate themselves more and try things they never thought possible.

We can become that positive voice singing in their heads long after we're out of their lives. That thing you said or did may get them through a difficult moment or may resonate with them for years.

A Winning Presence

One of the best ways of leaving a mark is to bring joy to the situations of life—light up the room. Some folks light up a room when they leave it. Don't be one of them. A friend asked me, "Are you always this happy?" I smiled and told him 95% of the time I am. The other 5% is the "happy" I want to be. It's an affirmation! So spend time trafficking in the positive thoughts that produce a winning presence.

We leave marks every day, and often don't even realize it. Let me prove my point. Have you ever had someone come up to you and tell of some great thing you said and you don't even remember it. They tell you how impactful what you said was for them and you say "Thank you," but you couldn't remember what it was you said. You accidentally left a mark. Miss Mattie would tell you to be more intentional and leave more marks.

There is no shortage of ways to leave marks. The more the mark lines up with who you are, the easier the mark will be for you to make and the more impactful it becomes.

Take 15 seconds and close your eyes. Think of someone who has made a difference in your life. Why is their name etched on your brain? What mark did they leave in your life?

What do you want the summary statement of *your* life to be? Do you want it to simply say you were just here? What is that? My mother would challenge you to live *a life worthy of your engineering*. You were made to win! You were made to be impactful, to leave a mark!

If you're reading this, I'm guessing you want your life to count. Live intentionally! Shannon L. Alder said, *"Carve your name on hearts, not tombstones."* When you're gone from people's lives, what will they remember about you? Will it be something you gave them? Will it be something you did for them? Will it be something you said to them?

Poet Maya Angelou said, *"I've learned that people will forget what you said, people will forget what you did, but people will never forget how you made them feel."*

We are all emotional beings. Make sure that your existence prompts people to feel something. Always make your marks so good, so indelible, so impactful that they will always remember how you made them feel.

I decided some years ago to honor my mother's charge to "leave a mark." I decided to live a life filled with touchpoints. After I have left, I want people to feel better because I showed up. Intentional living has become my mode of operation. I live to leave marks. Won't you join me? You'd make my mother smile!

MISS MATTIE'S PROOF

MISS MATTIE'S PROOF

*"Children are not things to be molded,
but are people to be unfolded."*
Jess Lair

We, Mattie's kids as we still are known, celebrate our births and our great nurturing and rearing compliments of Miss Mattie. You have read about her life and, at times, felt her pain. She was a woman to be celebrated and never pitied, no matter what life laid at her feet. In August of 1995, our mother passed away leaving an enviable legacy to the world. If she were here now, she would point to the validation of her commitment to her children . . . her Proof.

Robert "Sunny" Stephens

Robert, Miss Mattie's first born, graduated high school from the school we would all graduate from, the iconic Alfred E. Beach High School in Savannah, Georgia. He then entered college and earned a BA degree in Music Education from Savannah State University. For a few short years, he taught high school in rural Georgia just as our mother had.

The Vietnam war was raging, and he was drafted into the army and served a few years in South Vietnam. He returned home safely and uninjured and reassessed his life goals. Moving to New York, he returned to college to get his master's degree. Afterwards, he began to teach at Montclair State University. He would return to college to earn his doctorate degree in music. As you might have imagined, our mother was happy beyond words.

He moved on to assume a position as professor of music at the University of Connecticut. He would ultimately retire in 2019 as a fully tenured professor. He is married and is the father of three sons and has an incredibly beautiful granddaughter.

Edward "Mickey" Stephens

"Mickey," as everyone knows him, was Miss Mattie's second oldest child and looked most like our father. He too entered college, but he had to delay its completion for a couple of years. He would finish Savannah State University, earning a BA in Education. He taught junior high and high school just as our mother had. He expanded his educational aspirations and became an outstanding coach of the girls' basketball team at his school. After several years of teaching and coaching, he returned to college and earned his master's degree.

When he retired from teaching, his heart called him into politics. He was repeatedly elected to a seat as a representative in the State House of Georgia. He has served in that seat for ten years. Along the way, Mickey served on the Chatham County Board of Education, which served the Savannah metropolitan area.

As a state representative, Mickey single-handedly spearheaded initiatives that accounted for over twenty-five million dollars in grants awarded to Savannah State University. He personifies the word "Representative," as he has represented his district of Savannah in a most admirable way. On October 25, 2019, he was selected to be Grand Marshall in the Savannah State University Homecoming Parade. His family rode on the float with him, and we beamed as people along the parade route called his name with great admiration.

Mickey is married and is the father of a son and a daughter and three much-loved grandchildren. He always lovingly refers to the three grandchildren as his "heartbeats."

LaVerne "Bernie" Stephens

LaVerne, Miss Mattie's only daughter, finished high school and opted to go to college out of state, attending Hampton University in Virginia. She followed her older siblings and our mother and majored in Education, earning a BA degree. She would go on to earn her master's degree from Georgia Southern University.

She taught high school in New Jersey for a number of years. Eventually settling in Savannah, she worked as an administrator for the Chatham County Public Schools. She did well and was very well thought of. That fact comes as no surprise to any who know LaVerne and are aware of her quick intellect, her passion for excellence, and her Mattie-like attention to detail.

When our mother could no longer take care of herself, LaVerne assumed the gargantuan task of maintaining a fulltime job and taking care of our mother. Her care for Miss Mattie was exemplary. Our mother wanted for nothing as LaVerne lived in the land of personal sacrifice for several years. It should be noted that just as Miss Mattie's love drove her commitment to her five babies, LaVerne honored the pattern and was driven by love to provide our mother with the very best of care.

After our mother passed, LaVerne relocated to Florida and later retired as a very successful principal of an elementary school whose turn-around she engineered. She and her husband have a daughter and four grandchildren who occupy great spaces in their hearts.

Rufus "Butch" Stephens

I was the fourth of Miss Mattie's five children. I was one of "The Twins." I arrived in this world 30 minutes before my brother James, and we proceeded to perpetrate a fair amount of foolishness as we grew. When I finished high school, I also attended college at Savannah State University. Unlike my mother and my older siblings, I heard a different drummer and had no interest in majoring in education and subsequently teaching.

I would go on to graduate school at the University of Florida where I majored in Food Science. Leaving Florida, I took a position with Kraft Foods and began my career in the food industry. My life would take many twists and turns as I worked different jobs and even owned a distribution business that employed thirteen people. After six and a half years, I returned to the food industry and ultimately retired from a company I had been associated with for thirty years.

Along the way, I perceived and accepted a call to ministry and became an ordained Baptist minister. In May of 2015, I launched a new speaking business called Raisin' the Rufe Communications. That business has provided me with success on many levels. Nearly two years ago, two friends, Norm Wood and Lauren McGhee, and I formed a workshop training business called The Collective Training Group. The momentum of our relatively new business has been staggering.

My wife and I have four children and four grand-children. It will sound self-serving, but I will say it anyway. We have awesome grandchildren!

James "Jimmy" Stephens

James is the 30-minutes-later "baby" I spoke of earlier. He is Miss Mattie's youngest child and my 30-minutes-later twin. As we grew, you may have thought he was the oldest because he faced life chal-lenges that I actively avoided. I still see him in my mind's eye, playing catcher for our baseball team. Anyone who would squat behind a man with a huge stick waiting for another man to throw a 90 mph missile his way is a special kind of brave.

James's middle name should be "resilient." During the grammar school years, he suffered from asthma. His asthma attacks were debilitating, and he often missed out on school and other activities. But he weathered those storms, partly because of the skillful hands of our grandmother and partly due to his own fortitude and resilience. He has since outgrown the asthma.

James graduated from high school and went on to attend Florida A & M University. Of the five of us, James is the one who always had a bent toward all things electronic. That bent coupled with his academic focus at Florida A & M equipped him for a successful career at BellSouth where he worked for nearly 30 years before retiring.

He has three children and a loving grandson. Retirement opened the door for a happiness he could not have imagined. He misses no opportunity to lavish love on his busy, lovable grandson. Their time together is often lost in glorious moments on the playground, reading, and singing oldies.

. . . But wait, there's more!

Beverly "Bev" Roberts-Hamilton

While Miss Mattie gave birth to five children, she would maintain that she had another child who also could be called "Mattie's Proof." When I was about fifteen, Aunt Gladys adopted a three-year-old child named Beverly. She quickly owned the hearts of all of us at 1016 W. 46th Street. Beverly, who wrote the foreword to this book, is our cousin on paper but our sister in our hearts. She took great joy in hanging out with all of us. But as her foreword attests, she formed a special bond with her Aunt Mattie. Because her mother, Gladys, and her auntie were educators to their very core, Beverly wore the family brand and soon emerged as an articulate young lady who learned quickly and laughed easily.

She too graduated from Savannah State University and Georgia Southern University. She earned her master's degree from the University of North Florida. An excellent educator in her own right, Beverly, like us, is further living proof of the Mattie effect. Beverly is now an accomplished educator in Florida.

She is married, and she and her husband have two daughters who are actively pursuing professional careers.

MISS MATTIE'S FURTHER PROOF

MISS MATTIE'S FURTHER PROOF — THE LEGACY

While much of this book speaks to Miss Mattie's impact on her five children, what can't be overlooked is Miss Mattie's impact on her grandchildren. Some of her impact was direct for those old enough to have spent quality time with her. If she were alive today, she would fully embrace the lives of not only her five children and her niece but also her eleven grandchildren and thirteen great grandchildren and two grandnieces.

Through the indelible impression Miss Mattie had on all of us as her children, her effect has become far-reaching as we continue to live our lives in joy. She would be proud of our accomplishments, made possible by her many sacrifices, her encouragement, and her strength of character. Reaching into the next generation, her grandchildren and grandnieces are accomplished in many fields, including music, law, software design, finance, and education. They have demonstrated great business acumen, and, most importantly, are parents of unparalleled abilities.

The Miss Mattie epic is still being written by her five children, her niece, her grandchildren, her great grandchildren and grandnieces. The eight life lessons meted out in loving Miss Mattie fashion as shared here will continue to speak volumes about her effect through the generations of her family and the many children she taught.

THE EPILOGUE

THE EPILOGUE

It took me some years to really appreciate just how awesome our mother, Miss Mattie, was. So much of what she did was simply her order of business. There was no fanfare to her character posture, her victory moments, or her endless perseverance.

Miss Mattie could have easily slipped into the realm of self-pity, leaving her children to fend for themselves. She could have been focused only on the needs of her children and no one else's. She could have encouraged us to draw up battle lines between ourselves and our father.

She could have told us that college was not in our future, so get a job and call it a wrap. But she didn't do any of those things! In fact, she couldn't. It was not in her makeup to do anything but what I have chronicled here.

She did revel in the victory moments of her children and her niece, Beverly. If you gave her the time and you could stand the stories, she would tell you of great adventures in our lives.

She has left a legacy that is rich. Each of us, her children, niece, grandchildren, great-grandchildren, and grandnieces, have lived, are living, and will continue to live lives on the shoulders of Miss Mattie, and we are forever grateful.

It was not just our family who benefited from Miss Mattie's character, however. Her love for people beyond 46th Street was something of legend. She found it nearly impossible to walk away from someone who had a legitimate need, especially if it was a young person. She loved the nickname "Miss Steve" which came from the rural communities of Georgia. It was proof of her heart connections.

I hope at least one of Miss Mattie's eight Life Lessons has touched you. When you put even one of these lessons in action, watch what happens in your life. I would love to hear your success stories, which I am sure will be forthcoming.

May the love and wisdom of Miss Mattie embolden you to chase after the life that destiny has scripted for you.

MISS MATTIE'S LIFE LESSONS

1. *Education is non-negotiable (You will go to school.)*

2. *Self-image (Remember, you are something else.)*

3. *Laugh regularly (Life is funny.)*

4. *Encouragement (We are blessed to bless.)*

5. *Stand firm (When you have to.)*

6. *Faith has feet (God ain't sleep.)*

7. *Season your speech (Say it with flavor.)*

8. *Live intentionally (Leave a mark.)*

EIGHT QUOTES TO LIVE BY

"Age is a number that measures our place in time. It fails miserably at measuring our passions and our possibilities."
Rufus D. Stephens

*"Not one drop of my self-worth
depends on your opinion of me."*
Quincy Jones

"Nothing is as powerful as an idea whose time has come."
Victor Hugo

*"There is no greater agony than bearing
an untold story inside you."*
Maya Angelou

"It is not as important when you bloom as that you bloom."
Rufus D. Stephens

"We don't get better by chance. We get better by change."
Jim Rohn

*"You can have anything in the world you want if you help
enough people get what they want."*
Zig Ziglar

*"There is no passion to be found in playing small—
in settling for life that is less than the one
you are capable of living."*
Marianne Williamson

About the Author

Mr. Stephens is a native of Savannah, Georgia. He graduated from Savannah State University and pursued graduate degrees at the University of Florida and National Baptist Theological Seminary.

He has been married to his wife Cynthia for 22 years, and they have four grown children and four grandchildren. He is a former business owner, corporate executive, and an ordained minister of twenty-five years.

Mr. Stephens is the co-owner of The Collective Training Group, providing impactful training for individuals and corporations across the country. His passion for public speaking has been longstanding as he has lent his voice to eager ears for over twenty-five years. He has won numerous awards for his much-loved presentations including the Toastmasters Humorous Speech Award for the 127 club Chicago region.

In 2015, Mr. Stephens formed a motivational speaking business called "Raisin' the Rufe Communications." His empowering presentations are always intended to energize the listener toward personal appreciation and active accomplishment.

The United States Department of Energy, DePaul University Alumni Association, the National Hookup of Black Women, Kiwanis International, the Georgia House of Representatives, the S. P. Richards Company, Savannah State University, the Florida School Nutrition Association, and Delaware School Nutrition Association are among his appreciative audiences.

You can reach Mr. Stephens at www.raisintherufe.com and raisintherufe@gmail.com.

Made in the USA
Monee, IL
01 December 2020